To my parents who always wanted the very best for me. This book is dedicated to you for helping me grow into the person I am today and always loving me unconditionally.

To all of the children out there who are told to grow up and stop daydreaming—don't listen to them. Never let someone else's darkness keep you from shining bright.

www.mascotbooks.com

Princess Peppermint and the Kingdom of Swirls

©2018 E. Claire. All Rights Reserved. No part of this publication may be reproduced, stored in a retrieval system or transmitted in any form by any means electronic, mechanical, or photocopying, recording or otherwise without the permission of the author.

For more information, please contact:
Mascot Books
620 Herndon Parkway, Suite 320
Herndon, VA 20170
info@mascotbooks.com

Library of Congress Control Number: 2018907662

CPSIA Code: PRT0818A
ISBN-13: 978-1-68401-818-5

Printed in the United States

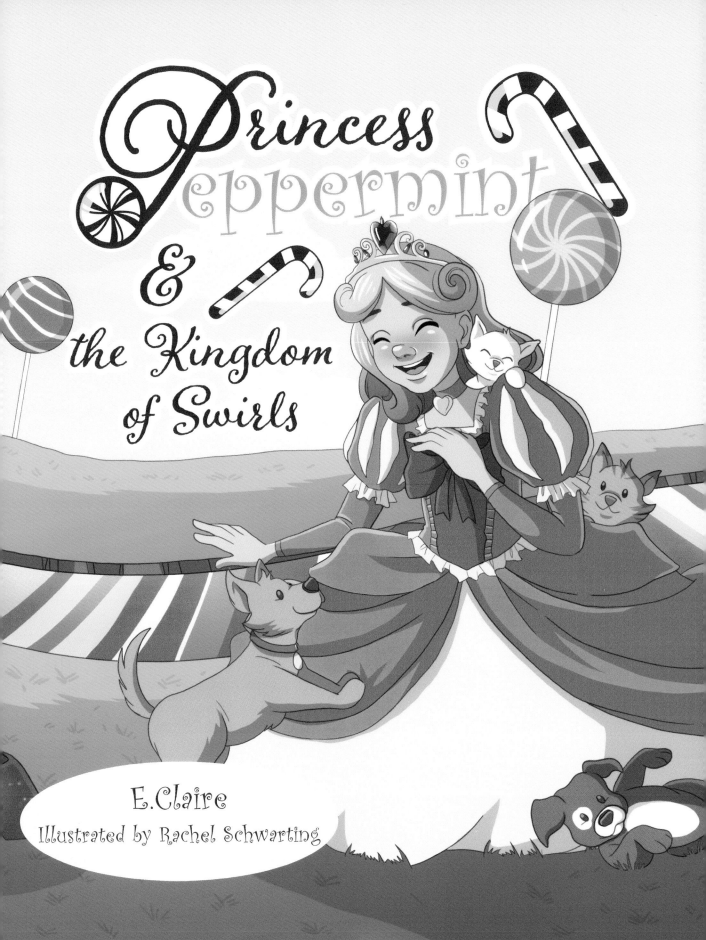

Princess Peppermint
& the Kingdom of Swirls

E. Claire

Illustrated by Rachel Schwarting

High atop the mountain past the birds and trees,
Up over the clouds where no one could see,
A castle stood still where candies ran free.

The Kingdom of Swirls was a land that was sweet,
From gum drops to kisses and all sorts of treats,
'Twas a magical place filled with creatures to meet!

The rulers were kind with love to share,
One King, one Queen who truly did care,
And one princess whose face was sweet and fair.

Princess Peppermint was loved by all.
With her beauty and kindness, her heart was not small–
In size, it could stand over ten men tall!

She would go on adventures, exploring the land,
From Gummy Bear Forest to Sugary Sand,
Seeing sights that were ever so grand.

Meeting all of those along her way,
Was Peppermint's favorite way to spend her day,
With wonderful friends with whom she would play!

The gingerbread twins were always fun.
They would jump and skip and laugh and run!
There was so much to do before the day was done!

Building miniature houses with Chocolate and Cream,
With sugary crystals, so bright they would gleam,
Shining like stars in a magical dream!

Cupcake Connie was always close by,
Making brownies, and strudels, and blueberry pies,
And she'd always make extra for Peppermint to try!

Continuing her journey down Lollipop Lane,
Princess Peppermint ran into Candy Cane—
Her best friend since the start of her reign.

They slid down an ice cream sundae, riding a spoon.
They played and played until they even saw the moon!
But the night was near and would be there soon.

It was time for the sweets to lay down their heads,
Time to go home, time to go to bed.
After the Queen read a story, "Goodnight," she said.

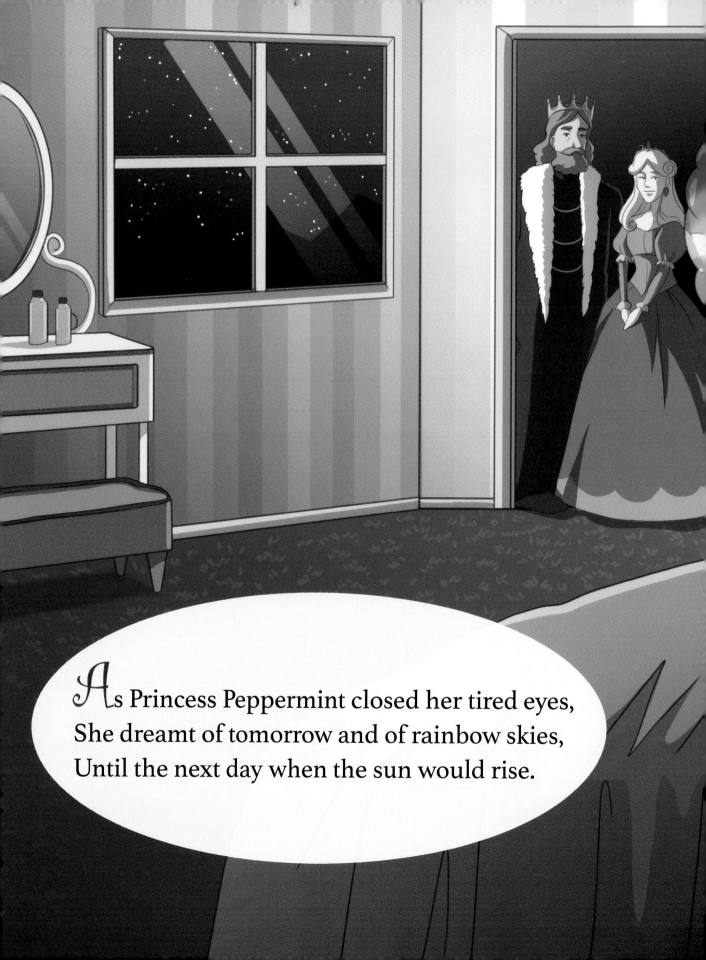

As Princess Peppermint closed her tired eyes,
She dreamt of tomorrow and of rainbow skies,
Until the next day when the sun would rise.

About the Author

Emily Claire Huneycutt is an industrial engineer by day and an author by night. As a graduate from East Carolina University, she holds a Bachelor's of Science in mechanical engineering. Working with many charities and organizations in her community, Emily has been able to use her passion as a volunteer to uphold many titles throughout her pageant career, with one of those being Mrs. North Carolina US Continental 2017.

During the national competition in 2017, she placed as first runner up in the Mrs. US Continental Pageant. Emily was always encouraged by her parents and family to use her imagination and dream big. This dream led her to writing *Princess Peppermint and the Kingdom of Swirls* and other short stories.

Her hope in writing these stories is that they will allow children to explore their creativity and imagination while seeing the world as a magical place. *Princess Peppermint and the Kingdom of Swirls* is Emily's first children's book.